ABC Facilitated Reading

Facilitated Learning

Facilitating learning fosters engagement, confidence, skills, accountability, character, voice, and relationship.

Dedication

For Rick Thompson, a smart, sensitive soul who didn't get the chance to live his best life as he never recovered from the brutal invalidation and humiliation he suffered at school before anyone knew about dyslexia.

Acknowledgments

Noreen Brigden and Jennifer MacAulay. I can't write a note for the bus driver without getting you two to read it first.

My Kids

Ryan, Morgan, Brennan, Ayden, Shayna, Erin and Julia.
I was 40 before I found my voice and 63 before I knew about facilitation. If I had known then what I know now, I would have done some things differently.
XO

Note to Facilitators

The picture book in Part One showcases the main sounds each letter represents but it is an incomplete list. The sounds **a** represents for example, are not limited to Ay as in *acorn*, a as in *apple*, or Aw as in *auto*. The **a** in *said*, *was* and *aisle* make different sounds again. The letter **c** usually represents k as in *cat* or s as in *celery* but not always. All three **c**'s in *Pacific Ocean* make different sounds. This level of detail about sounds doesn't help learners with the process of reading. The idea **that letters can represent many sounds is the lynchpin**.

Judy Thompson

ABC Facilitated Reading

AN INTERACTIVE SYSTEM FOR TEACHING READING AT HOME

All rights reserved. This work is the intellectual property of the author. This book contains material protected under International and Federal Copyright Laws and Treaties. No part of this publication may be reproduced, distributed, or transmitted in any form or by any means, or stored in a database or retrieval system, without permission in writing from the author, except in the case of brief quotations embodied in critical reviews and certain other non-commercial uses permitted by copyright law. All third-party trademarks referenced or depicted herein are included solely for the purpose of illustration and are the property of their respective owners. Reference to these trademarks in no way indicates any relationship with, or endorsed by, the trademark owner.

Thompson Language Center
Niagara, Ontario, Canada
www.ThompsonLanguageCenter.com

ABC Facilitated Reading
An interactive system for teaching reading at home.
Facilitated Learning Group www.linkedin.com/groups/14108606

Copyright © 2023 by Judy Thompson
Published by Thompson Language Center, Developed in Canada

First Edition

ISBN: 978-1-7781823-2-7

CIP available upon request.

Edited by: Ruth Taylor, Jennifer MacAulay and Noreen Bridgen
Design and Production by: McCorkindale Advertising & Design
Photos: Cover, pages 1, 3, 6, 60; iStock by Getty Images.

Printed in USA (subject to change)

 www.thompsonlanguagecenter.com

Table of Contents

PART ONE — 6
ABC Picture Book: The Letters of the Alphabet and the Sounds They Make

PART TWO — 60
The Facilitated Reading Guide

Backstory — 62
Introduction — 64

Chapter One: Tell the Truth — 65
Rules for Facilitated Reading — 65
Out with the Old — 65
In with the New — 66
Facilitators Need a Bit of Training — 67
The Nitty Gritty of the Facilitation Process — 69

Chapter Two: Work with Their Amazing Brain — 72
A) Noticing Patterns — 72
B) Attach New Information to Old — 74
C) Memory — 74

Chapter Three: Find Their Carrot — 75
Step by Step: The Learning-to-Read Process — 76
Why Dr Seuss? — 80
Alternatives Approaches — 83
Thompson Vowel Chart — 84
Approaches to Avoid — 85
Ending on a High Note — 86
Conclusion — 87
References — 88

Part One

ABC Picture Book: The Letters of the Alphabet and the Sounds They Make

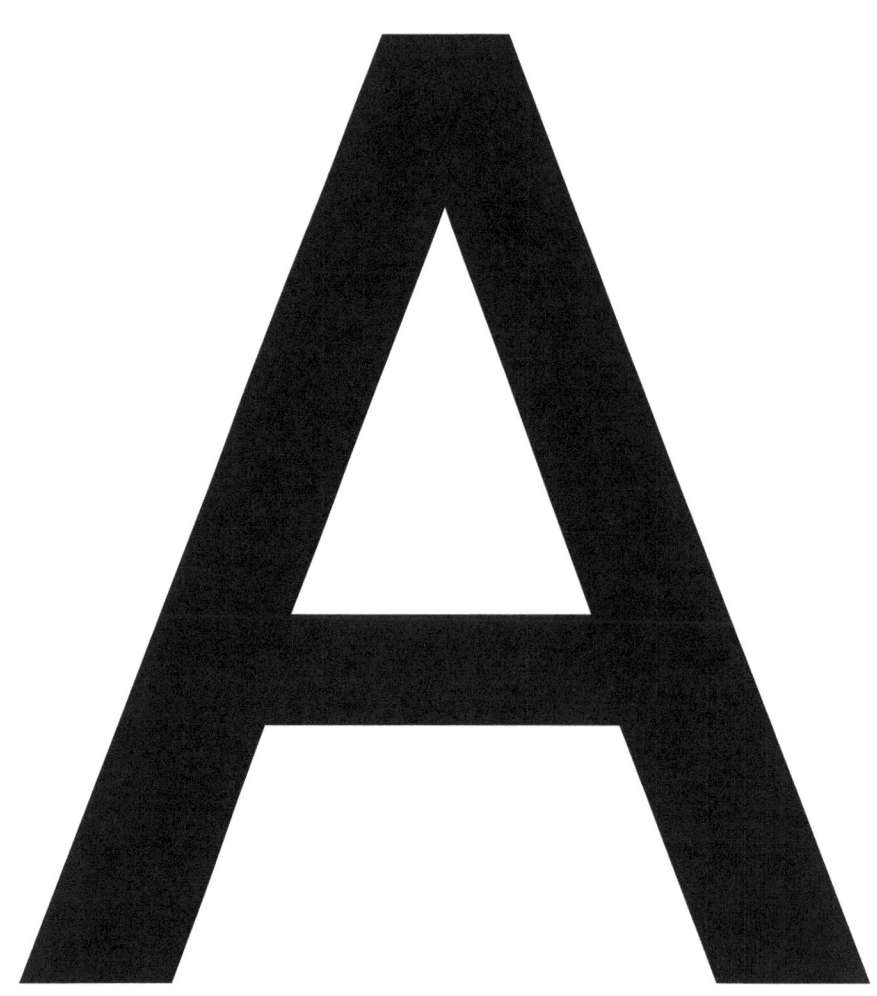

A is for **Acorn**

Ay

A is for **Apple**

a

A is for **Auto**

o

B is for Boy
b

C is for **Cat**
k

C is for **Celery**
s

D is for Dog
d

E is for **Ear**

Ey

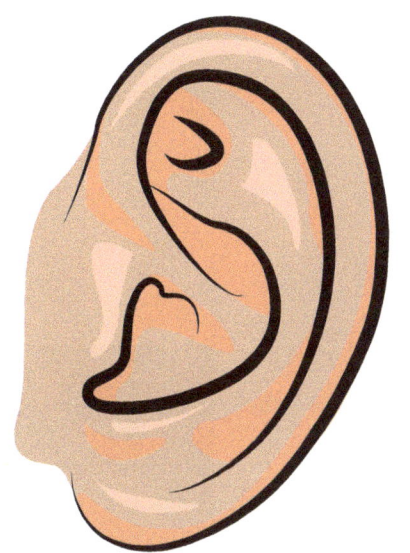

E is for **Elephant**

e

F is for Fish

f

G is for Goose
g

G is for Giraffe
j

H is for House
h

I is for **Ice Cream**

Iy

I is for **Igloo**

i

J is for **Jump**

j

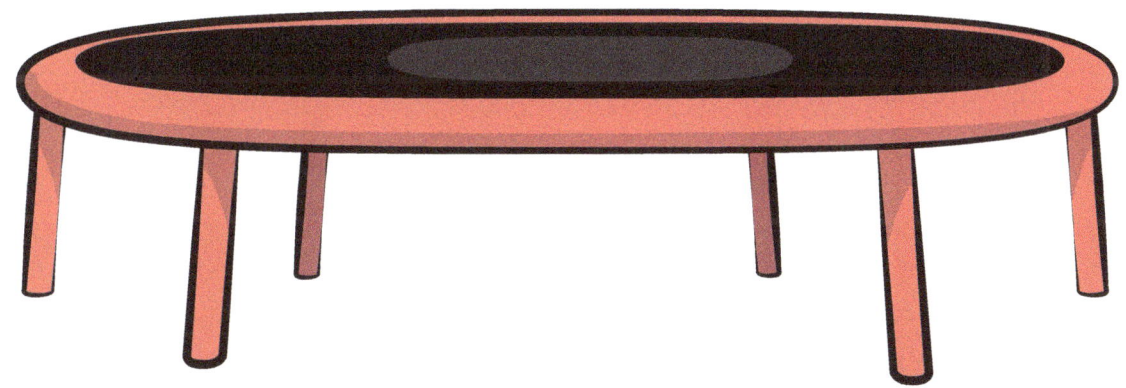

K is for **Kite**

k

L is for Lion
l

M is for Mouse

m

N is for Nurse
n

O is for Ocean
Ow

O is for Ostrich
o

O is for Owl
Aw

P is for Pig
p

Ph is for Phone
f

Q is for Queen

kw

R is for Ring
r

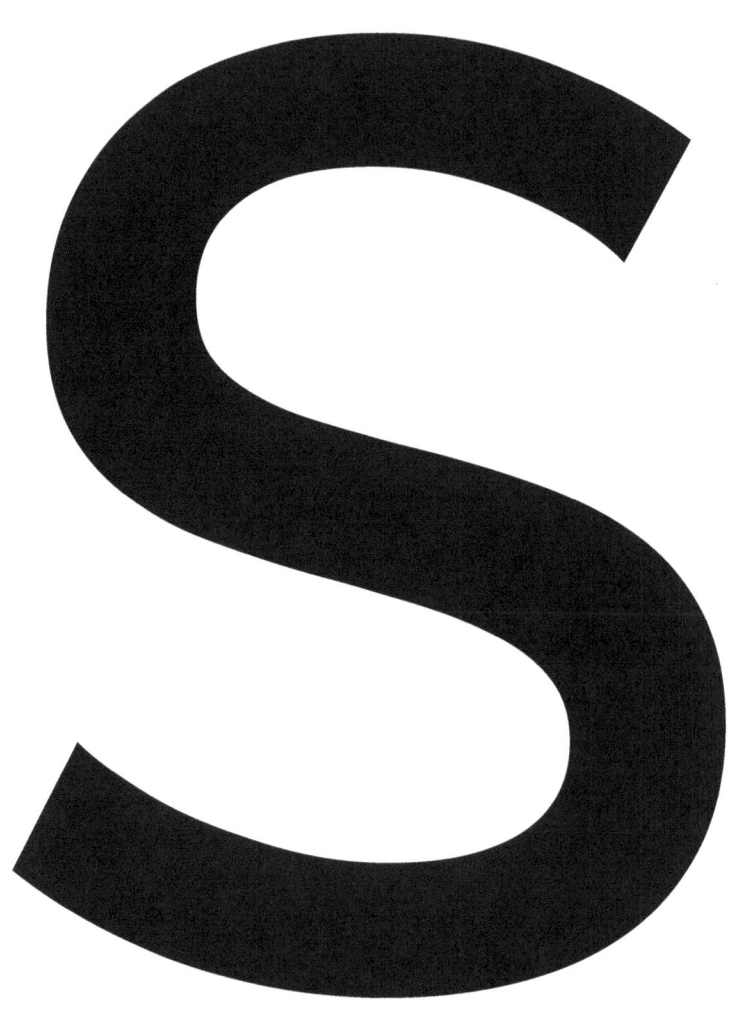

S is for Star

s

T is for Turtle
t

Th is for Thumb
Th

U is for Unicorn
Uw

U is for Umbrella
u

V is for Violin
v

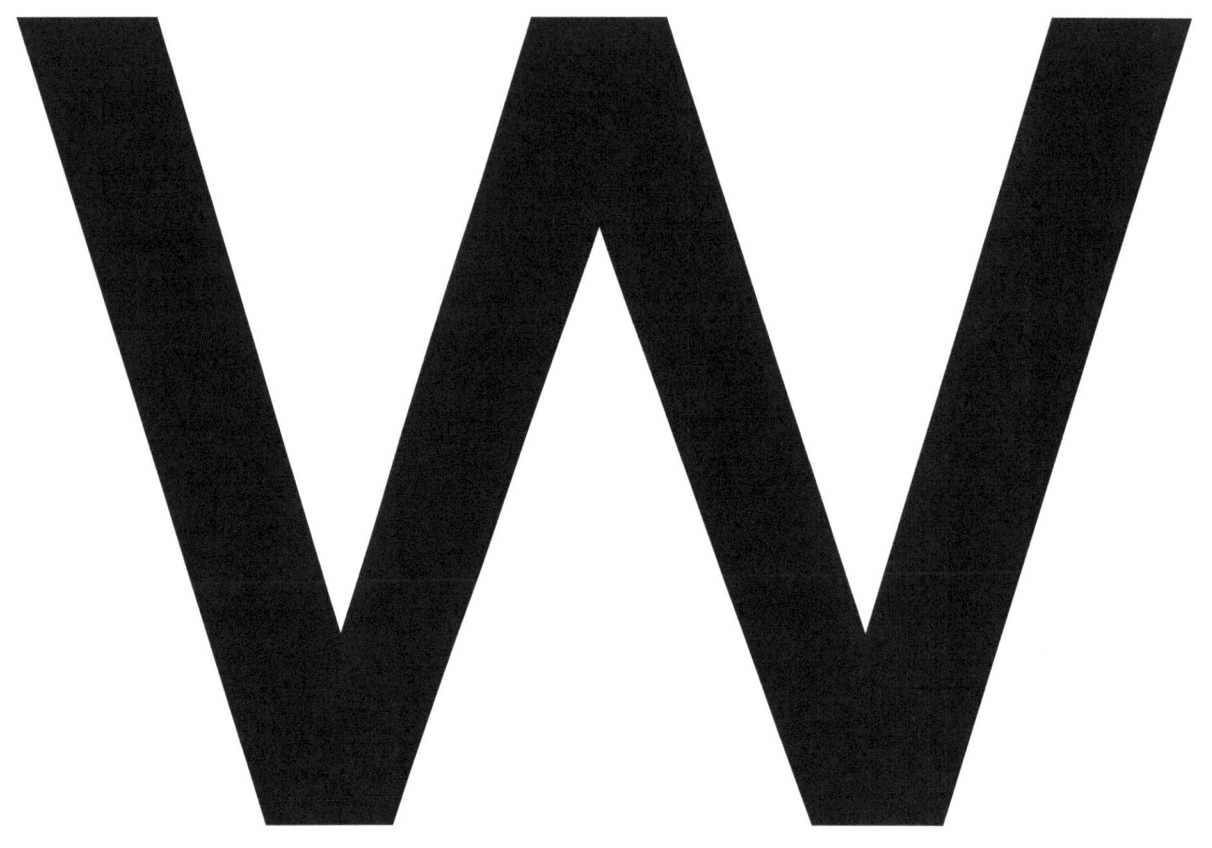

W is for Wolf
w

Wh is for Whale
w

X is for X-ray

ks

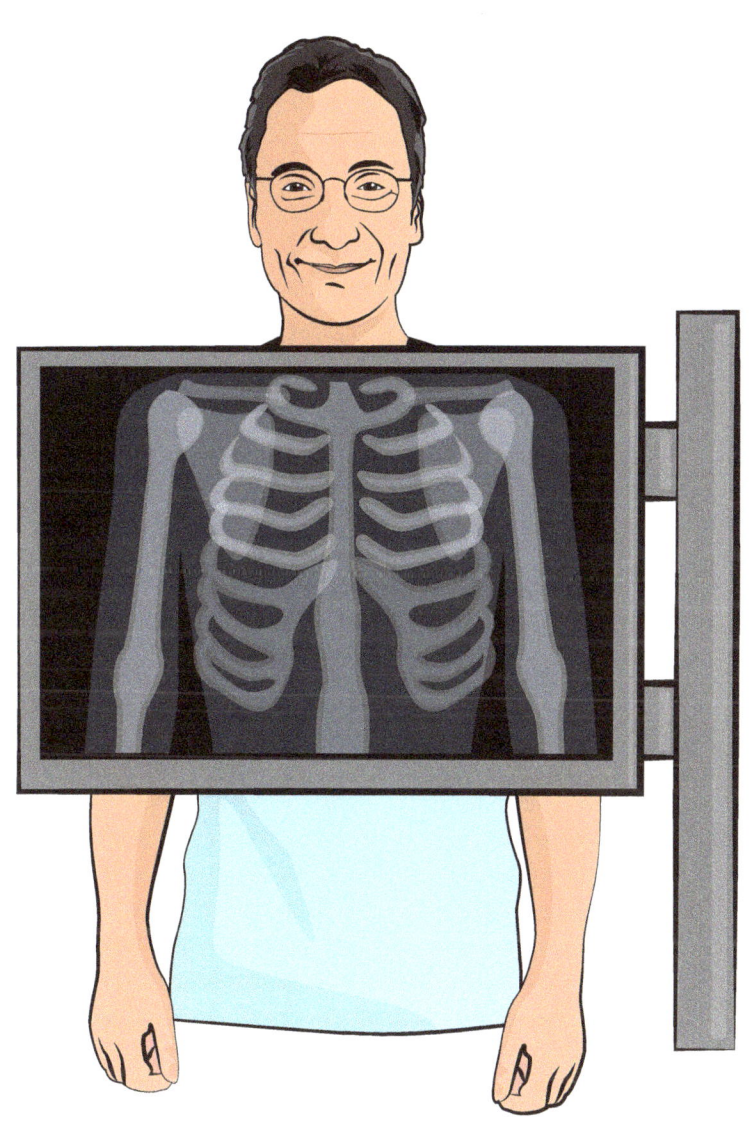

Y is for Yellow
y

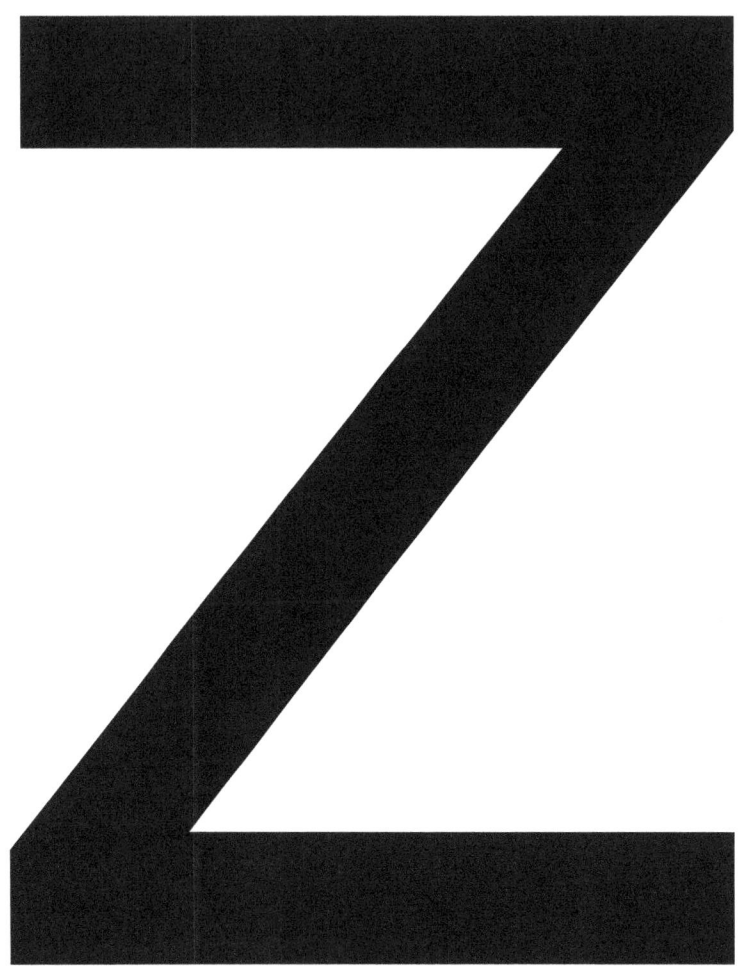

Z is for Zebra

z

Part Two: The Facilitated Reading Guide

Backstory

Difficulty reading is a big, expensive problem. *Thirty-six million Americans can't read well enough to hold a job.*[1] The problem English speakers face when **learning to read** English is twofold and, oddly, they are the same issues English-as-a-second language (ESL) students have **learning to speak** it.

Spelling doesn't make sense and **education fails to address it.**

With only 26 letters in the alphabet and 40+ sounds in English, there is no **direct correlation between letters and sounds**. Letters are very tricky little squiggles. They appear in different **styles** and fonts, and each one can represent more than one **sound** or be **silent** at any time. Once it is clear that the snag with English is **illogical spelling**, solutions abound.

My education career began teaching immigrants and refugees to speak English. Introducing my breakout book **English Is Crazy** (ne *English Is Stupid, Students Are Not*) at ESL events opened new doors, the most surprising was **reading literacy** for native English speakers. Conference attendees would approach me after presentations and ask me if I could help their child read? The anxiety and desperation in their voices was palpable. They often remarked that they knew their child was smart, which added to their pain and confusion. I did have suggestions for helping children read. The seed for developing a facilitated reading program was planted.

Anguished parents are right about their children being smart. *Many children with above average intelligence have difficulty learning to read.*[2] How can this be? The breakdown isn't with the learners; it isn't even with the teachers. The breakdown is with our **education system**. Blaming children as lazy, stupid, or not trying were go-to explanations for eons, but none of these excuses were true. The industry's failure to teach reading persisted partly because it was culturally inappropriate for parents to question authority and partly because there is no accountability in education. It is so much easier to simply blame the victims. It's **institutional bullying**. But bullying isn't acceptable anymore, not in schools, families, sports, industry, business, or politics.

In the likely event school fails to do it, parents, grandparents, and caregivers are perfect candidates for helping children to read. No one knows the strengths, weaknesses, and personalities of children like those who love and care for them. School is about academia. It is not there to develop happy, well-rounded, high-functioning members of society. School is not about individuals and it's fallible. Once families learn effective techniques, teaching children to read at home is viable and fun! Long-suffering parents can feel better now. We've got this.

The traditional approach to reading is awry. Reading isn't a collection of letters; **reading is a collection of sounds**. With no logical alphabet to guide them and therefore no reliable representation of sounds, **learners need a bridge** or a crutch to get from crazy spelling to reading comprehension. Once reading skills are established, the crutch can be thrown away. I use a simple **sound alphabet** as a bridge, but there are other methods for bridging random groups of letters aka words, to reading. (see page 83)

Don't be nervous. You don't have to learn or teach a phonetic alphabet, but you must make it clear that **letters and sounds are two different things**, like this:

Sounds are represented by letters in **red**.

This is a dog. It makes the sound **woof.**

dog

Woof

This is a **d**. It makes the sound **d** in **dog**.

This is an **m**. It makes the sound **m** in **moon**.

This is an **s**. It makes the sound **z** in **please**.

This is a **p** and an **h**. Together they make the sound **f** in **phone**.

Letters and sounds are different things, and reading is about sounds. Learners don't need to know a second alphabet for sounds; they need to know the names of the letters of the alphabet and that letters can represent more than one sound.

WHEN DINOSAURS ROAMED THE EARTH

How did I learn to read? How did you? For me the journey to understanding how reading happens began in 1963, Grade 1, Clarkson Public School, Miss Speck's class. I remember the exact moment I learned to read.

The word was **the**. I repeatedly stumbled on **the** by pronouncing it **t-he**. I could clearly see the **he** in it, so I was confident about that part. I just needed to add a **t** at the beginning. I was mistaken. "It's **thu**, Judy. Sound it out." The frustration in Miss Speck's voice mounted. I loved Miss Speck and wanted nothing more than to please her. By the third time I misread **the**, by sounding the **t** first and the **he** second, I realized **I could *sound it out* OR say it like Miss Speck wanted me to, but I couldn't do both**. I gave her what she wanted: **thu**. I uttered it tentatively. (The first two letters together make a sound neither one makes on its own, and the **e** makes a **u** sound as in up.) Miss Speck was thrilled, and that made me happy. **T·H·E** says **thu because Miss Speck said so**, and that was good enough for me.

> **Reading is a game and letters are loose sets of possible clues.**

I love games. Once I stopped trying to *sound it out* and began assimilating possible clues, I read so quickly and so proficiently they bumped me up a grade level. I had to carry my desk to my new class (of big kids) while my friends stayed behind in Miss Speck's class, desperately trying to *sound it out*. (I was traumatized, so were they.)

Fast forward 60 years to my granddaughter coming home from Grade 1. "My teacher says *sound it out*." I flipped out. **Nothing damages children faster and more completely than insisting they do something that can't be done, and then blaming them when they can't do it**. It is abuse. English is a non-phonetic language. No one can *sound it out*. It is possible to learn to read, but not that way. I was inspired to take on industrial education and create a more effective and more enjoyable system for learning to read. ***ABC Facilitated Reading*** was written for my granddaughter and for every heartbroken parent and grandparent who loves a smart child struggling to read.

Introduction

I was shocked and disappointed to discover education hadn't improved how reading is taught in over half a century. *According to the U.S. Department of Education, 54% of adults in the United States have prose literacy below the 6th-grade level.*[3] With at least 40% of high school students in English-speaking countries graduating **functionally illiterate**, something must be seriously wrong with the way reading is taught. It gets worse:

> *Two-thirds of students who cannot read proficiently by the end of 4th grade will end up in jail or on welfare.*[4]

Got it! The consequences are astronomical, and the chances are excellent that your child may not learn to read in school. This is not the teachers' fault. In my experience, teachers work hard and really care. The problem is the way reading is taught. **Teachers have no training in teaching reading effectively**.

IS THERE A BETTER WAY?

The process where one all-knowing individual imparts information to underlings who are required to absorb that information, then regurgitate it on a test at some future date, is deeply flawed. Psychologist Hermann Ebbinghaus gave us the **forgetting curve** in 1880. He determined how quickly information is forgotten—roughly 56% in an hour, 66% after a day, and 75% after six days.[5] While these findings are staggering, it's even harder to accept that education in North America today is delivered in exactly this format more than 140 years after it was proven to be ineffective.

Outside North America, the education picture is brighter. Scandinavian countries adopted a **facilitated** Study Circle model with stellar results. *The key causes of Nordic prosperity and quality of life are... solid public primary and secondary education.*[6] Finland is also consistently ranked the happiest country in the world, possibly because *facilitated learning* not only produces academically superior results; it is enjoyable! Facilitation values individuals, fosters empathy, and builds community. It is an exciting and efficacious way of learning.

TEACHERS TALK, FACILITATORS LISTEN

The difference between teaching and facilitating is profound. Teaching is so ineffective, we aren't going to do it. We are going to facilitate instead. Facilitate literally means to make a process easy or easier. In broad numbers, teachers talk 80% of the time and facilitators talk 40%. As a reading facilitator, plan to spend quality time engaging with learners in a new, interesting, purposeful way.

> **When you teach a child, they hear your voice;
> when you facilitate a child, you hear theirs.**

It's a game worth playing.

RULES FOR FACILITATING READING

1) Tell the truth.

2) Work with their amazing brain.

3) Find their carrot.

Chapter One: Tell the Truth

Facilitation has three general rules. You'll learn these rules and see how to apply them, but first we have to clean up our work space.

OUT WITH THE OLD

Tell the truth seems obvious until we realize we don't know the truth. We only know what we were taught. Misinformation is sewn into the fabric of our way-we-have-always-done-it system. As thinking and questioning are not parts of industrial education, we can only pass on the misinformation we received.
Do any of these whoppers sound familiar?

- **Sound it out.**
- **I before E except after C.**
- **Two vowels go walking, the first one does the talking.**
- **A before consonants, and AN before vowels.**
- **Silent E makes the vowel say its name.**

Don't take my word for it.

Sound It Out

If you look at it, *sound it out* is nonsense. Numbers 1 to 9, for example:

1 wun, **2** tuw, **3** threy, **4** for, **5** fiyv, **6** siks, **7** seven, **8** ayt, **9** niyn

Less than 5% of English words are spelled the way they sound.

Is and **his** sound like iz and hiz.

Was is pronounced wuz.

Of sounds like uv.

Little is lidul

There, they're, their: thayr

I, eye, aye: Iy

Air, Aire, ayre, ere, err, Eyre, heir—ayr—at least seven different spellings with the same sound and different meanings!

The most common words in English are the most crazily spelled or spelt.

I Before E Except After C

With more than **6,000 exceptions**, *i before e except after c* is not a rule—a rule of thumb maybe. Weird, weight, eight, height, beige, neighbor, vein, forfeit, heist, sleigh, glacier, and foreign, are but a few.

So how so many adults get caught up in repeating garbage? And with such conviction! Sir Ken Robinson was knighted for saying, **Schools kill creativity**, but he was being polite. Schools destroy our ability to think for ourselves.

Two Vowels Go Walking
When two vowels go walking, the first one does the talking? It isn't true. Millions of should-know-better educators and parents thoughtlessly repeat this, and it hurts learners. *Of the top 2,000 most commonly used words in English, only 36% follow the rule. 64% do not.*[7]

Look at the vowel pair **EA**, which makes 15 different sounds in this incomplete list of examples; then never mention vowels walking again: **meat, great, head, earth, react, heart, create, acreage, area, beau, beautiful, Sean, Roseanne, sergeant...**

A or AN
A goes before nouns that start with consonants and **AN** before nouns that start with vowels. Everyone knows that. What about **a unicorn, an honor, an hour, a one-eyed cat, a European, an M, an F, a U**? Something is not right.

As mentioned previously, **reading is sounds**. Never mind spelling—spelling is nuts. The rule is ***A** before nouns that start with consonant **sounds** and **AN** before nouns that start with vowel **sounds***: a yunicorn, an onor, an our, a wun-eyed cat... a yeropean, an em, an ef, a yuw. A/AN is not a spelling thing; it **is** a **sound** thing.

Silent E Makes the Vowel Say Its Name
Not necessarily, and there's the rub. The brain abhors exceptions. **Any 'rule' followed by its exceptions is not a rule** and confuses learners. At best, *sometimes silent E makes the vowel sound say its name.* The **not always** is the problem.

Love, are, come, have, some, one, there, gone, sure, where, done, give, live, move, whose, there, were...the list is **infinite**.

Enough with the unlearning for now.

Are you beginning to wonder what else we learned in school that wasn't true? Good! The answer is lots. (Christopher Columbus did not discover America.) Feel free to challenge anything you read or hear from now on—in this book, in the news, on social media, in life. If you get nothing else from this book, be open to looking at education and what others tell you, with fresh eyes.

The beginning of **telling the truth** is to stop repeating untruths.

IN WITH THE NEW
Facilitated learning is an interactive, customized process which is emotionally, physically, and technically different from the traditional method we are familiar with.

Emotionally Different
First and foremost, let the learner know how **capable they are**. Industrial education recognizes *smart* as how quickly a student grasps and regurgitates *what the teacher has told them to think*. Intelligence is understood more broadly now.

Learning isn't a race; it's an individual process.

English is complex; you don't ever want a learner to think there is something wrong with them. There isn't. People learn in different ways at different rates. Facilitation is emotionally different from indoctrination because the learner is the main event in their learning journey. Their **individuality** and their **opinions matter**.

Physically Different
Learning by doing sets facilitated reading apart. Learners are encouraged to engage, contribute, question, point, trace, match, and make mistakes. In conversation with their facilitator, learners **experience** teamwork, patience, persistence, fun, compassion, and critical thinking. Social skills underpin academic skills. Autonomy flourishes as a direct result of the student's active participation in their own learning.

Technically Different
ABC Facilitated Reading is different and better because it provides an authentic array of the most common sounds each letter makes. When a learner encounters an **A**, for example, they can draw from several likely options. **A** probably makes one of three sounds: **<u>a</u>corn Ay**, **<u>a</u>pple a**, or **<u>a</u>uto o**. When exceptions crop up (s<u>a</u>id, for example, where **A** makes an **e** sound), learners can manage because the system has prepared them to consider a range of possible alternatives. *ABC Facilitated Reading* is honest. **Trust learners with the truth**. The elasticity of human intelligence is more than capable of managing the elasticity of English spelling.

FACILITATORS NEED A BIT OF TRAINING
People see the world through filters shaped by their personalities and experiences. No two people understand the same thing in exactly the same way.

Allow for differences. As a parent, grandparent, or caregiver, take the time to understand and accept the learner's perspective and guide them toward the lessons they need to move forward.

Do you see a musician or a girl's face?

> It is possible you have never experienced this level of acceptance and consideration personally. Be kind to yourself. We are all learning.

Basic Facilitation:

1) VALIDATE: Listen to and value all contributions.

2) INTERACT: Question, reassure, compare, discuss.

3) REGULATE: Manage the time and the direction of each session.

4) CONTEXTUALIZE: Show how small parts fit into the big picture.

You will get a sense of facilitation from these examples. The theory follows.

The A Page
On the **A page**, ask the learner, "Do you know what the first picture is?" In the unlikely event they hit the jackpot and say **acorn**,

> **Validate** – "Great!" Then move on to the next picture.
>
> It is more likely they'll say, "I don't know," or not respond at all.
>
> **Validate** – "That's okay. I didn't know what that was either when I was your age."

67

They may also say a nut or a brown thing. *These are not wrong; they are just not the answer you were going for.*

Validate – "That is a nut!" or "It is a brown thing!"

Interact – If they didn't know what an acorn is, chat it up. Nuts are tree seeds. Acorns are seeds from oak trees. It's an **acorn**. Interaction goes both ways, through questions and answers. Not on the first day, but soon you can look things up with the student: "I'm not 100% sure about this. Let's look it up." Be vulnerable. Model how you learn new things.

Regulate – A chatty child may want to tell you everything they know about trees or nuts or brown things. Smile, acknowledge, and rein them in gently—"I can see you know a lot about trees" or nuts or brown things or whatever—and move on.

A quiet child is thinking. This is good. Silence can be uncomfortable for adults. Get over it. Hold space for their thinking.

Contextualize – We need a word that starts with an **Ay** sound, so we are keeping **acorn** for this picture.

Learners usually get **apple** right away, but if they don't, use the same process.

How about the third picture?

They may say car. It is more likely they will say *toy* or *lawn mower* or *I don't know*.

Validate – "Yes! That is a car" or "It does look like a toy" or "I saw a lawn mower that looked like that."

If they don't know—awesome. Honesty. *I don't know* is a perfectly acceptable response.

Interact – Feeding learners information is sometimes appropriate. It's an old-fashioned car. An old-fashioned name for a car is an **auto**. Perhaps they've seen a car like this in a movie or in a parade?

Contextualize – We need a word that starts with the sound **o** like in **olive** and **octopus**. **Auto** starts with the sound **o**.[8]

On the **D page**, when you ask the learner what they see, they are very likely to offer *a puppy*. It's not wrong.

Validate – "Yes, that looks exactly like a puppy!"

Interact – "Can you think of another word, one that starts with the sound **d**, that this picture could be?"

Regulate – The learner may say **dog** and go on to describe a dog their cousin had... Bring them back onside with tact. "My cousin had a dog, too." Back to task.

Contextualize – For the **d** sound, we need to remember this as **dog**.

> Your pupil is learning the sounds of the English alphabet, and they are also learning *cultural dialogue conventions* by having conversations and sharing their ideas in a space you have made safe for them.

THE NITTY GRITTY OF THE FACILITATION PROCESS

1) Validate

Facilitation stretches our ability to put ourselves in another's shoes, to see and accept that seeing things differently is fine, and normal. It begins with **listening**. Being listened to is a form of validation.

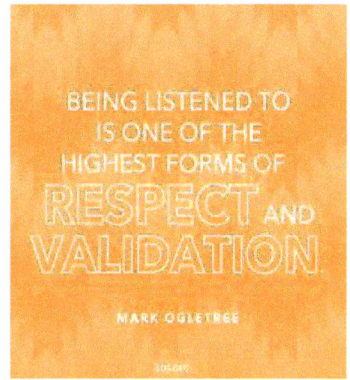

After listening, make positive remarks to acknowledge each contribution. "I never thought of it like that. You have a great imagination..."

Facilitated learning is not about getting to the right answer as quickly as possible. It is about **thinking**. Engagement, contribution, conversation, validation, context, and noticing patterns cultivate thinking. **Thinking is a messy non-linear process.** At this stage, **ignore mistakes.**

Learners enjoy the time you spend with them. They contribute, are heard, validated, and encouraged. FUN! Oh yes, and they learned! This is a game children will play!

> It is possible you have never been truly heard. I'm sorry. This level of engagement and listening may be a new experience and require new skills from you. You are going to trip up sometimes. That's okay. Try again. You can do it.

2) Interact

By **accepting all contributions**, you create a space where the child can say whatever they are thinking. The safer they feel, the more confident they become about contributing and the less concerned they are about making mistakes. Humans learn from asking questions and making mistakes. Facilitation uses both.

The Context for Contribution

Timothy R. Clark describes four stages of psychological safety.[9] The first is **belonging**, the learner feeling they are in the right place. The second stage is **learning**. People can't learn if they are uncomfortable. The student hasn't necessarily said anything yet. When they feel safe enough to **contribute**, you will know they are at the third stage. At the highest level of personal security, a learner will feel safe enough to **challenge**. Remember this when your student disagrees. When you hear some form of "I don't think so", take a deep breath and pat yourself on the back for creating the ultimate safe learning space.

The Context for Mistakes

Facilitating is not about stepping over mistakes—far from it. Mistakes are important and inevitable. Embrace them. Think of errors as learning opportunities.

Mistakes are not bad; they are a necessary part of learning.

There is tremendous value in how you react to mistakes. Shaming, threatening, or punishing have no place in facilitated learning or anywhere.

> **Walk Your Talk**
>
> The most powerful way to handle mistakes in general is to own your own. We all make them. "I made a mistake. I'll try again. Sorry about that."
>
> Personally, **I can't spell.** This shortcoming of mine is frequently evidenced on the board in front of a class. Students are encouraged to point out my mistakes to me. "Thanks for helping me. I appreciate it." Learners take more away from your example than anything you tell them.

Accepting imperfection is grace. With facilitation, children gain confidence, voice, and grace while learning to read!

3) Regulate

As facilitator, you manage the length, frequency, and quality of sessions. If possible, regular, short, engaging sessions are more effective than sporadic long ones. Five to fifteen minutes, five or six times a week is in the ballpark. You'll soon get a sense of the learners's working window and how long they can enjoyably and productively focus. It fluctuates if they are tired, sick, or upset. When they stop bugging you to play the *Reading Game* with them, listen up; something may need to be addressed.

Beware the babblers. Learners bask in your attention and may not want to go to bed. If you're not careful, worthy little opponents can hijack time spent together to further their own agendas. Within reason, don't hand over complete control.

Talking isn't always good, and silence isn't always bad.

After 2.5 seconds of dead air, adults feel compelled to fill the space with noise. *Westerners have a cultural intolerance for silence.*[10] To assuage our discomfort, we may repeat the question or offer clues. While it is difficult to wait in patient silence, **wait in patient silence we must**. The learner is thinking. They need time. Be mindful of your own false sense of urgency that demands quick, perfect answers.

There is *thinking silence* and *bored silence*. Body language tells the difference. Resist the temptation to fill the air with noise too quickly when a learner is thinking. Resist the temptation to ask for more effort when the child can't concentrate—one more page or five more minutes. Respect their limits. It is okay to stop in the middle of a page when they are full and losing interest.

Some of the perks of learning to read at home are the customization available from knowing your child's limits and your own, managing schedules, and eventually choosing the materials to read!

4) Contextualize

Contextualizing is about **perspective**. The facilitator knows the big picture and the relative weight of individual pieces to the whole. There are bigger fish to fry than minor errors. What education jumps on as a mistake is more powerfully embraced as a contribution or an approximation. Sometimes, it's appropriate to completely ignore mistakes.

Teachers see what is wrong.
Facilitators see what is right.

Context and interaction offer better choices for advancing the plot than always nit-picking. More important than getting something perfect as quickly as possible is having learners know that who they are, how they think, and what they have to say matters. Emerson saw something I didn't see on the L page.

BUDDING FACILITATOR PRACTICE MOMENT

You are on this page of the book and ask the four-year-old on your lap, "What's this?"

And he says, "*It's a seven.*"

What do you say?

Think about it before you read my suggestions.
Hopefully you didn't have to think long.

"Yes, that is an upside down seven!"
"I didn't see it like that. I was thinking about the animal and the letter. What animal is this?"

"*Lion.*"

"Yes! And the letter L."

The sound l for lion is what we want to remember from this page.

"Good job."

Chapter Two: Work with Their Amazing Brain

We don't have to be neuroscientists to understand the basic workings of the brain. Brains naturally A) **notice patterns**, B) **attach new information to old**, and C) **remember**.

A) NOTICING PATTERNS

The human brain is a pattern-seeking, meaning-making machine.[11]

This is true of all people in all situations. The pattern for washing is getting it wet, agitating with soap and rinsing. Maybe drying it too. The pattern for driving vehicles is once you know how to start it, how do you make it go, steer and stop?

Patterns are **things that repeat in a logical way**. Patterns help humans make predictions because they can anticipate what comes next. Patterns help humans make logical connections and use reasoning skills—in other words, **think**.[12]

We can't stop our brains from seeking patterns. Use it. Reward learners not so much for regurgitating or memorizing, but for making connections on their own that weren't pointed out to them. This is thinking. Reward learners for thinking, not for simply guessing what you want or hope they'll say.

> Rewards for thinking rather than for correct answers is a different way of looking at objectives. Facilitators may need to cultivate this new skill.

Here are some examples:

In the fresh excitement of learning the shapes of letters, learners start finding these shapes everywhere! Five-year-old Avery picked up a stick in the yard and exclaimed, "Look, a Y!"

Yes! Great noticing.

ABC books provide code words with the focus on the first letter. However, when learners begin to notice letters elsewhere in words, it is even better. With no prompting, they may say **p** or **l** like **apple**. "Yes, the sounds **p** and **l** are in apple!" That is a brain leap. Validate that.

After a few sessions of *The Game*, Alyssa paused on the **K page** and exclaimed, "Like Rick!" Absolutely. The last sound in **Rick** is **k**. She wasn't wrong. She was sorting sounds out. She was thinking. Reinforce approximations and any timely guesses on their journey.

> **The Truth Is Subjective**
> In my experience, all children are smart in their own way and right given their experiences. This mindset helps me get past insisting on my way and move on to understanding the path the child's mind took to draw their conclusion.

On the **Q page**, I mention that **Q** always shows up with **U** as a partner, queen, quiet, quarter, question.... On the **T page**, Jacy commented, "**TH** like **queen**." *Yes!* They had made the association of two letters working together as partners. Don't be too quick to decide they are wrong. People will work hard for you when you believe in them.

You can appreciate how much more enjoyable a student's learning experience is when they are not repeatedly invalidated for incorrectly guessing what is in the instructor's head.

When you consider the way a child's amazing brain is assimilating data, you'll realize all their responses are correct (unless they are tired or just being silly, as children sometimes are). Learners find patterns and attach new information to information they already know. The facilitator's objective is to see how their answers are accurate in the context of their experiences.

> ### Give Pause
> When you encounter an opinion completely different from your own, the secret is to stay open. If you don't immediately understand a connection someone has made that contradicts your reality, **ask questions**.

The pattern for reading is 1) memorizing the names of letters and most of the sounds they represent 2) identifying individual words 3) processing groups of words working together to represent ideas 4) comparing new information to old as in rejecting the new information as folly or incorporating it into our belief system. Is there anything humans do that isn't based in patterns?

Toxic Thinking Alert!

It's hard to imagine that our minds do not always serve our best interests. Unfortunately, there is a widespread pattern in human behavior, rooted in childhood beliefs, when our brains work against us. Children accept everything trusted authorities tell them as true. Think parents, teachers, priests.... If information received as a child is inaccurate or incomplete, not only do we continue to hold it as truth, but we also defend that misinformation to the death. It shakes us to the core to learn Christopher Columbus never made it to America, much less discovered it. It's like our whole lives have been a lie. It is the stuff of disagreements and wars.

The Evil Twins – Cognitive Dissonance and Confirmation Bias

Cognitive Dissonance – Western culture can't process new information that contradicts long-held beliefs. We feel compelled to ignore or invalidate evidence that challenges what our moms or our Miss Specks told us. Cognitive Dissonance is why the fake story of Christopher Columbus became a national holiday and why **I before E** and the gang continue to haunt education.

Confirmation Bias – This twin goes one step further and selectively collects evidence that overvalues or supports our claims and minimizes contrary evidence. It's why conspiracy theories abound. A few minutes on the Internet can supply us with support for ANY twisted myth we choose to believe.

The evil twins account for the same political and religious affiliations surviving generation after generation within families, with no consideration for alternatives, changing times, conditions, or facts. The real enemy isn't someone who thinks differently but our own human impulse to defend our beliefs simply because we were told to believe them when we were very young.

We can't think our way past information we internalized as children, even when that information is wrong or no longer serves us.

Confirmation bias and cognitive dissonance are adult burdens. To some degree, we all have them. Once we are aware of these afflictions, the way past them is a combination of thinking and courage. Get used to considering that there is a difference between the truth and what you believe.

It takes extraordinary courage to face down and let go of long-held beliefs.

> Not everyone can do it. That you have read this far in a book that challenges what you believe about learning to read speaks volumes about your character and your open mind. I'm proud of you.

B) ATTACH NEW INFORMATION TO OLD

The *ABC Song*[13] is a perfect example. The order of operations for **learning to read** is first to identify the names of the building blocks—the letters **A B C D E**... The *ABC Song* holds the information necessary to start the reading process. Children as young as two or three can sing the *ABC Song*. The song's value is in labeling letters, and **putting shapes to the letter names learners know from the song**. This is hard work.

The *ABC Song* exists as a reference until learners eventually memorize the names of letters and can name them without prompting. What comes after **P**? They'll sing the song from the beginning to find **Q**. It's a great resource for orienting 26 essential pieces of information. Children's minds love thought-anchors like the *ABC Song*.

Once learners know the names of letters, the next critical step is to learn that letters represent sounds. The thing that's wrong with all ABC books except this one is that they offer only one sound per letter. This misinformation is incredibly destructive.

C) MEMORY

Memories are like pathways through a dense forest. The more often you take a particular route, the clearer and easier to follow that path becomes. It is difficult to find your way through a forest you have only traversed once or twice. Huge advantages in the beginning are luck and attitude. We don't have much control over luck, but the willingness to try over and over again can be encouraged. Be patient. Give learners time.

Repetition serves memory. Presenting the same basic material in different, interesting, and fun ways reinforces learning pathways. *ABC Facilitated Sound Flashcards* are useful here.

Chapter Three: Find Their Carrot

A) Find what **motivates** each child.
B) **Stop before** they are sick of it.

Children love being with you. While your attention and validation are valuable to them, these aren't reasons enough to work as hard as they need to in order to read. So, pay them. Stars, grapes, Smarties, tokens toward a baseball game a tractor ride or a special activity—use whatever motivates them. (*Smartie* is a euphemism for a treat or reward in this text.)

Mikaela is a brilliant little girl who didn't feel like playing *The Game* and wasn't interested in treats or anything else I offered. But when her little brother played *The Game* and she saw him get rewards, she couldn't stand it. She's competitive. There is nothing wrong with that. The point is, find their trigger, their gold, their carrot. They have to want to play *The Game*.

Be careful about rewarding a learner for simple memorization unless it's extraordinary. Don't fall into the trap of giving treats to your child because you love them so much and need to believe they are superior human beings. They are, but now is not the time for that. I don't reward a seasoned learner for remembering the names and sounds of letters, but I reward a beginner for that.

You have a sense of what lights your child up. I use Smarties in those little boxes. A single Smartie is the perfect-sized treat, and holding the box in their little hands is a heady incentive. There are nine or ten Smarties per box, which is a reasonable number of successes per session. Smarties work well for a ridiculous number of children. Older learners are motivated by other incentives.

Reading Is Its Own Reward

Whether or not it is a good idea to *pay someone to read* is a controversial topic as one dad found out after posting this message on Twitter.

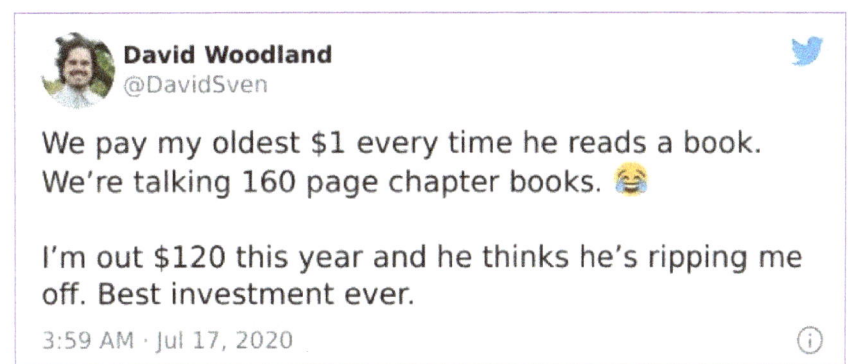

It is not so much a case of paying learners to read, which is fun, but of paying them to learn to read, which is hard work. In my experience, once a learner can read, they don't look for other rewards. David Woodland's son told his parents they didn't have to pay him anymore, and I find this is usually the case, but it's your call.

The ABC Game

In its initial stages, learning about letters and sounds isn't reading any more than Monopoly is a course on real estate investment. But reading and property investing are skills players can acquire from playing games. What is traditionally known as *teaching a child to read*, I call *The ABC Game*. Because learners are developing skills by finding clues in pictures, shapes, and code words, assessing data, and making their best guess in order to procure rewards—it is a game.

Step by Step
LEARNING-TO-READ PROCESS

Step One – The Names of the Letters

The ABC Song is ground zero. It teaches the **names of the letters** in an effective and entertaining way. The names of the letters anchor reading skills.

Step Two – Attaching Sounds to Letters

Facilitated reading diverges here from other reading programs. This is the letter **A**. **A** makes a few sounds, usually the Ay in <u>a</u>corn, a in <u>a</u>pple, or o in <u>a</u>uto.

> **A Lucky Break**
> The beauty of the first letter of the alphabet representing more than one sound is that **A** addresses the fundamental reading challenge on the first page. **Letters can represent more than one sound**.

Depending on the learner's age and prior exposure to the alphabet, introduce them to four or five letters and their sounds in the first session with the book. (Pages 8-15)

Start the next session (later the same day or the next day is ideal) by reviewing the letters they have seen. "What letter is this?" Be patient. Tolerate mistakes. Reward tiny increments of learning. **Stop before** it isn't fun.

Too often adults are governed by some secret agenda that has nothing to do with the learner. "There are only two more Smarties. Let's keep going." "Bobby got to page 10 on his first day. Let's keep going." Push, push, push—this isn't cool. The learner's journey is about them and nothing else. Not you, not your agenda, not anyone else—them. And they are perfect and amazing exactly as they are. However far they get in a session is perfect.

Big A, Small a

Together with the names of letters, traditional education introduces capital and small letters from the outset. Facilitated Reading doesn't do this because it isn't necessary at this time. Learners have more important things to process first. After they can read, students easily accommodate an infinite range of lettering shapes.

$$
\begin{array}{ccccc}
\text{Aa} & \textit{Aa} & \mathfrak{Aa} & \mathscr{Aa} & \text{Aa} \\
\text{Gg} & \textit{Gg} & \mathfrak{Gg} & \mathscr{Gg} & \text{Gg} \\
\text{Ss} & \textit{Ss} & \mathfrak{Ss} & \mathscr{Ss} & \text{Ss}
\end{array}
$$

Sadly, while school pushes capital and small letter shapes, it **never mentions** the really important issue with letters, which is their loose relationship to sounds. The vagaries of letters and sounds, the assimilation of clues in order to read, building character, voice and relationship are our priorities. In this program, students do learn capital and small letters, various shapes of the same letters, punctuation, indentation… eventually. It doesn't serve learners to distract them from what is important by introducing noncritical conventions at the beginning of their journey. That said, if they are exposed to capital letters and small letters at the same time, it isn't a big deal.

Step Three – Letters That Look the Same.

Learners often stumble on letters like **M**, **N** and **W**. They are probably noticing the up and down bumps. If they confuse letters, still acknowledge first, discuss, and then make adjustments. "Good job. I see what you are doing. You noticed the bumps in **M** and **W**. I used to mix them up, too. Now I remember **M** is like a mountain, and **W** is like water."

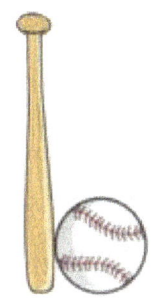

When learners do encounter small letters, they may struggle with **b/d**, or **p/q**, for obvious reasons. An oral description or a quick sketch can help them out: **b** is stick up and a circle. Draw a sketch of a **bat** and a **ball** in the shape of a **b**. **d** is circle and a stick up. "Now that you mention it, they really are similar." Tracing the letters with a finger or on a piece of paper is also a good support exercise. Mixing up letters doesn't make someone stupid or dyslexic—just a learner.

Step Four – Working with Sounds

Hello *ABC Sound Flashcards*! Flashcards are great. They become comfortingly familiar and can be used in a variety of ways. Download the *ABC Sound Flashcards* pdf from the Thompson Language Center website and print your own set. (See page 88)

Use six or seven cards in a session grouped: **A–G**, **H–N**, **O–T**, **U–Z**. For reasons that are now clear, when looking at the code words you can't say "sound it out," but you can say, "**Let's look at the sounds**." Let the learner casually identify any letters, sounds or words that they can.

Consonants are much stronger clue letters than vowels. It is far from a perfect correlation, but consonant sounds have a much stronger connection to letters than vowels do. The mind is looking for patterns, and vowels don't have any. Stepping over vowels at this stage is something to consider. Focus on stringing the consonant sounds together until the learner recognizes the word—or not. Next time is fine if it doesn't happen now. Stop worrying.

I was playing *The Game* with five-year-old Rowan who was very clever at guessing code words from the pictures. This is fine; this is what they are there for. But she was stumped on the **N page** with **Nurse**. She knew the name of the letter **N** and the sound n that it made, but looking at the picture she said, "I don't know what this is." "**Let's look at the sounds**," I encouraged. Running her finger under the letters she said, *n r s*, then paused. "Nurse," she said loud and clear. Smartie. It was the first word she had truly read, and it was music to my ears.

N is for Nurse

Vowels are a nightmare. Languages from the great grandfather of the English alphabet (Phoenician 700 B.C.) to modern texting function successfully without them. It's okay that students rely more on consonants when learning to read and add vowel awareness when learning to print.

Step Five – Independent Words
Flashcards again. You can make your own *ABC Word Flashcards* for the code words in the book or print the pdf download from the Thompson Language Center website (See page 89).

Set the ABC Picture Book aside. Lay out the first six or eight *ABC Word Flashcards* in an orderly grid. For the most novice students, you can lay the cards in alphabetical order— it's your call. I usually place them slightly out of order. See if the learner can identify any of the words on the flashcards. There is no prompting or discussion about words at this time. Remembering words without the picture is hard, and they may not get any of the words. No biggie. Identifying words uses a different part of the brain from the one they have been using so far.

Up until now, they have focused letter by letter in words. The skill of word analysis is performed in the parietal-temporal region of the brain. The name of it doesn't matter. (It's an oversimplification to say different areas of the brain have special roles without adding that many parts of the brain collaborate constantly in the reading process.[14])

What matters now is that recognizing the word as a whole with its meaning and saving words in a storage center happens in the occipital-temporal region. Learners are starting to make brain connections that will help them store words as meaningful units for quick retrieval in the future. The more words stockpiled in this center, the more fluent a reader they will be.

Acknowledge their effort with a Smartie for each word they remember. It might be one or two or none. It doesn't matter. Without further ado, give them the book. Finish the session by having the learner place the flashcards in the book on the correct pages. I give them a Smartie for completing this task. Matching the word on the flashcard to the word in the book is fairly easy. They will probably do it all from the first letter alone. That is fine. They can end the session feeling supported and triumphant.

In subsequent sessions, add more flashcards. The learner's brain may consider the shapes of the words—long words, short words, tall and short letters...It is harvesting data and generating its own set of clues. Their mind will work out its own pathways with repeated exposure to the material. Your job is to facilitate by making memorizing code words a fun, interactive, and positive experience.

Step Six – Word Association
Some learners appreciate using the code words for letters in the same way pilots use *Alpha, Bravo, Charlie* to identify letters. Word association is a **memory tool**. *Cat, Apple, Turtle* can be a crutch learners use to connect letters to spelling or pronunciation. Not all minds embrace this crutch. If this isn't sticking with your pupil, let it go. It doesn't matter in the least. You can be sure their amazing brain is figuring out a system that works for them.

Step Seven – Match Game
Hand the learner the entire set of shuffled Word Flashcards and have them **match each one to its page**. Smartie. Give them all the time they need. They love this activity, especially if they don't need help. It does wonders for their confidence and self-esteem. What looks like free Smarties to them is really *repetition play*,

refamiliarizing themselves in a casual way with the shapes and sounds of letters and words, **reinforcing** budding pathways through the dense forest.

Step Eight – Rudimentary Reading

They are making the leap to processing whole words versus letter-by-letter. Spread out *ABC Word Flashcards* **A** to **L**, slightly out of order. "Do you know what any of these words are?" Don't expect them to answer immediately. Give their amazing minds the opportunity to find paths.

Pay the child a Smartie for every word they can figure out. It may be only one or two words this time, but they'll probably get something. "Yeah! Good job."

Look at the remaining words together. You can prompt them by looking at the individual sounds. "What sound can this letter make? And this one?" Don't torture them. **The book is a resource. They can look in the book if they want to**. It astounds me how often learners don't want to look in the book; they want to mentally work for it. People are amazing.

> **C·A·T** – **k a t** – Guess – Cat – Perfect! Smartie. This is not reading yet; it's educated guessing. Even better.

Rudimentary reading is guessing. You are supporting their ability to remember bits of information, assimilate clues, and make good guesses. Reward reasonable attempts, not just quick random offerings. The program is about learning to read, not about dispensing treats like a vending machine.

If the student offers the wrong word but it starts with the right sound (a friend's name, such as Caitlin, may pop up here). Yeah! It's a positive. "Yes, that is another **k** word but not the one here." **Discerning correct approximations and acknowledging them is facilitating**. It makes the learner feel good about themselves and want to keep playing. Don't worry about being perfect. It is about time spent, reinforcing thinking paths, and storing word units.

Step Nine – Beyond the Book

If this hasn't come up organically already, spell their name and the names of other members of the family, then their friends and words outside the classroom. I remember sitting in the car and my mother hitting the brakes. I idly noticed **S·T·O·P** on a red octagonal sign beside the car. The penny dropped. "That says Stop!" It was the first word I read without Miss Speck.

Not necessarily in the first week, but soon, it's a good exercise to add new words to the letter pages. "**m** is for **M**ouse. Can you think of any other words that begin with **m** like **M**ouse?" Give them a minute to see what they say. "Mommy" is a common response. Smartie.

When you spell their pets' or friends' names with them, you are giving them more and more anchors to connect new words to. The brain loves these. It takes a long time to retrieve sounds from shapes, and they will have to think back on all the data they have been exposed to so far. You know where I'm going here—they need a bit of time. Guesses are still encouraged. Mistakes (I struggle with that label) are opportunities to more clearly understand where they are coming from and, most importantly, they are not the end of the world.

Step Ten – Beginner Reading

You have created a great bond, a safe enjoyable space, a perfect environment for the main event: reading. **Dr. Seuss** is your new best friend. Not just anything he produced and not in just any order. There is tremendous value in experiencing Dr. Seuss in this order. *Dr Seuss's ABC, Hop on Pop, One Fish Two Fish Red Fish Blue Fish, Green Eggs and Ham*, and *The Cat in the Hat*. These are the books, and this is the order that pulls learners forward to happy, successful reading skills.

Why Dr. Seuss?

Dr Seuss's ABC

There is an incredible amount going on in *Dr Seuss's ABC*, all of which works with the learner's mind. Here is a partial list:

- Illustrations that are silly, consistent, **engaging**, and effective.
- Loads of scrumptious **repetition** in alliteration, rhyme, style, and content.
- Exposure to the most common words' crazy spellings.
- Organic introduction of capital and small letters, including typeset **a** and **g**, which may be new to learners.
- Capital letters, or BIG letters written in a large font.
- *BIG* and *little* printed in a different color than the other words on each letter's page is a reinforcement that is subtle and creative.
- Illustrations that include **body language**, which heavily support meaning and **context** in literature and life.
- A spattering of nonsense words that force all readers to focus on and **think** about reading: a duck-dog, googoo googles, Fiffer-feffer-feff...
- Steep **progression** in difficulty to include multisyllabic words—alligator is on the second page and Zizzer-Zazzer-Zuzz is on the last.

Dr Seuss is the ultimate learn-by-doing experience. In many cases, when nothing about reading is explicitly taught, children learn to read when Dr. Seuss is read to them repeatedly.

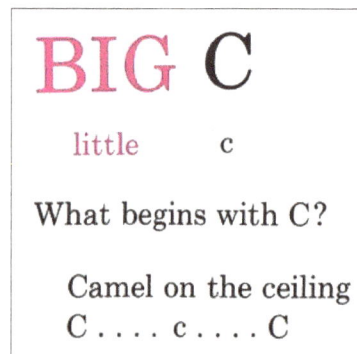

Camel on the **c**eiling, C represents **k** and **s** in the same sentence. It's **telling the truth**, working with the brain, and making reading fun.

By accident or design, "Camel on the ceiling C....c....C" is one of the most powerfully subtle and enlightening phrases in English. The same letter represents different sounds in the flow of content. Word list: 133

Hop on Pop

Hop on Pop uses many of the techniques we have come to expect from Dr. Seuss, with a few extras.

- A focus on families of rhyming words with similar spellings and sounds.
- Opposites (day/night, up/down) that offer practice in predicting from pattern.
- A vowel sound featured on every page (see the Thompson Vowel Chart[8]).
- Liberal switching between words printed entirely in capitals or in small letters.
- Silent letters and consonant blends.

Children often memorize *Hop on Pop*, internalizing common words and building print vocabulary. Word list: 150

One Fish Two Fish Red Fish Blue Fish

One Fish Two Fish builds on the myriad lessons of *Dr. Seuss's ABC* and *Hop on Pop*: repetition of common words, engaging style, and rhythm.

Adjectives are a special feature of *One Fish Two Fish*. Every word is important in written English, but that isn't the case in spoken English. It is surprising, but adjectives are more important when we speak than the nouns they describe. Adjectives are spoken with more energy. Check it out:

One fish, two fish, red fish, blue fish.

This phenomenon is part of a larger pattern in spoken English: some families of words (we won't go into them now) are pronounced with more energy than others. There is also a slight pause between small groups of important words when they are spoken. *One Fish Two Fish* showcases pausing and inflection (the up and down in reading aloud). Word list: 112.

> *From there to here, from here to there, funny things are everywhere.*

The brain took a giant leap during reading infancy from analyzing letters in words to recognizing whole words and storing them for future use. It takes another leap forward in *One Fish Two Fish* to interpreting strings of words working together to convey more complex ideas.

From *One Fish Two Fish* forward, groups of words become sentences, sentences become paragraphs, paragraphs become chapters, chapters become books, books become libraries… Each step builds on the one before, through the magic of reading. You can plot your child's mastery of reading on this continuum.

Green Eggs and Ham

On a bet that he couldn't create a story using only 50 words, Theodore Geisel (Dr. Seuss) produced *Green Eggs and Ham*. He inadvertently gave us an ideal stepping-stone to independent reading. Rife with familiar sight words, repetition, rhymes, goofy illustrations, and a great message, his trademark fantastical *Green Eggs and Ham* is often the first book children read on their own. And they are more than happy to read it to you or anyone who will listen, over and over again. Success! It is no wonder *Green Eggs and Ham* is consistently among the top-selling children's books of all time.

The Cat in the Hat

Everything we've looked at and more are gems in *The Cat in the Hat*. How does that devil, *sound it out*, fare in real life? Let's look. The letter **O** shows up 15 times in these two stanzas and makes four different sounds:

> I sat there with Sally.
> We sat there we two.
> And I said, "How I wish
> We had something to do!"
>
> Too wet to go out
> And too cold to play ball.
> So we sat in the house.
> We did nothing at all.

In **go**, **cold**, and **so**, letter **O** makes the same sound: Ow – Gold in the Thompson Vowel Chart.[8] (It isn't necessary to learn or use this chart, but check it out for yourself as a resource.)

In **two**, **do**, **too**, and **to**, letter **O** makes a different sound: Uw – Blue

In **something** and **nothing**, a different sound again: u – Mustard

In **how**, **out**, and **house**, yet another sound: Aw – Brown

There are four different sounds with little consistency in spelling.

> *But that is not all.*
>
> *Oh, no.*
>
> *That is not all...*

Tiny two-letter words that should sound the same, don't. To and do rhyme with each other but not so or go.

The letter **A** is as bad as the letter **O**.

Acorn A	play Ay – Gray
Apple A	sat, Sally, and, had, at a – Black
Auto A	ball, all o – Olive
Elephant E	said has an **A** that makes the sound e – Red

Word list: 236

This better be the last word spoken in support of phonics and *sound it out!*

Miracle of Miracles

Every foible and pitfall of crazy English spelling can be unraveled by our minds without instruction. That's right, the miracle of miracles is that about 5% of people learn to read from repeated exposure to books like *The Cat in the Hat*. Humans are learning sponges.

It can't be stressed enough. Regular reading to learners fosters their literacy.

> *The single most important predictor of academic success is the amount of time children spend reading, more important even than economic or social status.*[15]

If you aren't a strong reader, don't have the aptitude, or can't make time, find a surrogate reader. Life is going to go better for learners if they are read to regularly. You know how they ask for the same book to be read to them every night for weeks and weeks? Do it!

Alternative Approaches

In round numbers, 80% of kids will learn to read with this system. But all is not lost for the ones who don't. There are some excellent alternative approaches, all of which incorporate **telling the truth**, **working with their brains**, and **having fun**.

The Logic of English, Denise Eide

Phonics is Kool-Aid, with one notable exception: Denise Eide and *The Logic of English*. Eide designed the only good phonics program I have ever encountered. While 108 may seem like a lot of rules, they are all true and they effectively explain 98% of crazy English spellings. For example, **no words end in V Q or J** is a rule; ***igh* always sounds like Iy** is a rule. Denise Eide is a pattern seeker extraordinaire and appreciates the sound base of reading. Her rules are easy to learn. They stick because they are 100% true and she makes learning them fun. I highly recommend *The Logic of English*, especially for young learners. http://www.logicofenglish.com [16]

BrainWare

This is another exciting reading program I endorse. BrainWare is especially useful for older students who have slipped through the cracks and internalized their struggle with reading as a problem with them. It isn't. BrainWare uses crutch clues (diacritic marks) to help learners over the hump of *I can't do this* with tremendous results. http://www.mybrainware.com [17]

Sight Words

I'm a fan of sight words to a degree. Here are a few: **all, am, are, ate, do, no, so, too, the, was, is, his, please, pretty, who**. It shouldn't take you too long to notice that you can't sound any of them out.

all, am, are, ate	– four different pronunciations of **A**
do, no, so, to	– should rhyme but don't, so something is wrong
the	– we talked about **thu**
was, is, his, please	– **S** is **z**
pretty	– the **E** makes an **i** sound, and the **T**'s make a **d** sound
who	– the **W** is silent

If sight words speak to the profusion of crazy spellings in the most common words in English and help build the storehouse of reading vocabulary, I can see the value.

Tactile

Making the letters large and having learners trace them with their index finger sends a letter-shaped message into the learner's hand, up their arm, and into their waiting brain, bypassing reliance on sight, which isn't always dependable. Tactile is a tip I used to give the tormented parents who approached me at ESL conferences. The International Dyslexia Association uses this as well as other effective techniques:[18]

> *Dyslexia is a neurological condition caused by a different wiring of the brain. There is no cure for dyslexia, and individuals with this condition must learn coping strategies. Research indicates that dyslexia has no relationship to intelligence. But some say the way individuals with dyslexia think can actually be an asset.*

The smartest people I've ever known are dyslexic. I'm thrilled research has shone some light on this fascinating condition and, to a large degree, destigmatized it.

Color Association

The *Thompson Vowel Chart (EPA Vowel Chart)* is a tool I made for ESL students who wrestle with pronouncing English because of crazy spelling. There are 16 vowel sounds in General American (GA) English, and each one is featured in the name of a color. **Judy is blue**, so are glue, you, two, do, news, juice, school and beautiful... **Every word in English is one of the colors in the chart**. To keep pronunciation independent of spelling, students file words in their storage center by color.

I have never used this chart to teach anyone to read. That said, I have received loads of positive feedback from people who do! Caleb is an older student, excellent at math and other subjects but didn't get reading. His mother heard about the Color Vowel Chart and shared it with Caleb. It made a huge difference for him. People report that students who have struggled with reading like to categorize words in a reliable, retrievable way. So, there you go.

Thompson Vowel Chart

Color Word	Color	EPA	Double Example
gray	(gray)	/Ay/	rainy day
black	(black)	/a/	black cat
green	(green)	/Ey/	green tree
red	(red)	/e/	red head
white	(white)	/ly/	white knight
pink	(pink)	/i/	pink ring
gold	(yellow)	/Ow/	old goat
olive	(olive)	/o/	hot coffee
blue	(blue)	/Uw/	blue shoe
mustard	(mustard)	/u/	honey mustard
wood	(brown)	/^/	good wood
turquoise	(turquoise)	/Oy/	noisy toy
brown	(brown)	/Aw/	brown cow
purple	(purple)	/Er/	purple girl
charcoal	(charcoal)	/Ar/	dark charcoal
orange	(orange)	/Or/	orange door

 © English is Stupid, Students are Not — Exercise Manual

The Cooper Combo

Creative Diacritic Clues – It is possible to customize any or all of the techniques covered here to suit your learner. Logan was a different kettle of fish all together. Logan had a fantastic school with fantastic teachers, but they were not able to help him read. They could only apply with great patience the same industrial, dysfunctional approach over and over again. They couldn't adapt to the way he learned, so he was a lost cause. COVID came, and his mother made a system to help Logan learn to read. She noticed he knew the flashcard sounds but **he couldn't hold on to the sound featured on the flashcard and transfer it to a new context** like a book. She made a special set of flashcards that incorporated aspects of the sound the letter represented. **W** makes the sound w—like water—with droplets of water and a puddle under the word **Wet**. If Logan lay the diacritic clue words on the page he was to read, he could remember the sound. **When the special clue card was removed, he could remember the word**. He reads. One smart mom made a special bridge for Logan to connect sounds with letters and words.

When he went back to school, she created a little video https://livingoutloud.education/ [19] to show his teachers what he had been doing. I was thrilled when I watched the video to see what she had done and couldn't help noticing that her system stood firmly on the three pillars: **tell the truth**, **work with his brain**, and **make it fun**.

The Menu Game

One little guy randomly got words wrong that he'd read correctly many times previously. Was he was reading or guessing? He was at my house for lunch, so I quickly made a set of 20 food and drink flashcards that included milk, juice, soda, pancakes, apple, bacon, broccoli, potatoes, steak, chicken, wraps, sandwich, chips, ice cream, peas, carrots, and ham.

The game is this: For his lunch, I make whatever items he selects from the flashcards.

He approached the task in exactly the opposite way I would, which would be to read every entry and choose from the entire selection. He knew what he wanted to eat and looked only for those words: pancakes, bacon, and juice. Done. He was definitely reading, not guessing.

Approaches to Avoid

Phonics and Whole Language

Phonics is the education system's insistence that spelling is logical, but it isn't. *Whole Language* is akin to waving a magic wand. The long-standing debate between Phonics and Whole Language—known as the *Reading Wars*—doesn't consider that they are both bad. *Balanced Literacy* combines elements of bullying from the first and fairy dust from the second. It is the most popular approach in America today. Although reading scores have improved significantly[20] in our cognitive dissonance–induced coma, they fall a long way short of good.

More American children suffer long-term harm as a consequence of reading difficulties than from parental abuse, accidents, and all other childhood diseases and disorders combined. In purely economic terms, reading-related difficulties cost more than the wars on terrorism, crime, and drugs combined.[21]

Teachers work hard inside a broken system that has absolutely no idea how to teach reading. It guts them. My heart breaks for students and for teachers.

Word-Shape Recognition
This approach uses the shape of the envelope around a word. I've never used it and I don't endorse it, but I stop short of saying it can't help anyone.
www.docs.microsoft.com/en-us/typography/develop/word-recognition[22]

Synthetic Language
Made-up words, or *Synthetic Language*, is popular in Great Britain right now. In a long history of epic education fails, Synthetic Language is by far the most ridiculous thing I have ever encountered. Avoid it at all cost.

Ending on a High Note

Teachers Who Changed Our Lives
Ask anyone to tell you about a teacher who made a difference for them, and they will not tell you about facts they learned. "Mr. Brown taught me Paris is the capital of France and it changed my life." They will tell you about an experience. We remember the *feeling* of being heard and *validated*, of some teacher-overlord seeing something special in us that we couldn't see in ourselves. It wasn't a thing back then, but we now recognize these as moments not of being taught but of being *facilitated*.

Tell us the story of a teacher who changed your life. **www.linkedin.com/groups/14108606** We'll start with one of mine. In Grade 5, we were learning about weights and measures. At the end of the lesson, Mrs. Stafford asked the class which weighed more: a pound of feathers or a pound of lead? The class chuckled and most of them raised their hands for the pound of lead option—obviously. A few overthinkers suspected a trick and put their hands up for a pound of feathers. Then she asked who hadn't put up their hand? Me—and I was the only one. I was shaking I was so terrified to be singled out. "Why didn't you put your hand up, Judy?" In my head I can still hear the kindness and support in her voice. "I think they weigh the same," I responded. "Good girl, Judy!" She let me go out for recess early.

I learned two things that day: when you get out for recess early, there is no one to play with; and one person can be right while everyone else is wrong. *And that has made all the difference.*[23]

Conclusion

Congratulations to the rookie facilitators who tried something new!
It took courage to decide to help a child read, and I venture you both picked up some new skills. Facilitating is a gift that keeps on giving:

Children will be kinder because of the kindness you have shown them.

They will be empathetic listeners because of the time and patience you invested in listening to them.

They will exchange opposing opinions without invalidating others because they experienced looking at things from many sides as a positive thing, with you.

They will try harder because you taught them to believe in themselves.

They will learn from their mistakes because they saw you own yours.

They will lend their voices to making the world a better place because you let them know how much their opinion matters.

They will engage wholeheartedly in mind-blowing conversations for the rest of their days because you facilitated their reading.

Facilitated Learning

Facilitating learning fosters engagement, confidence, skills, accountability, character, voice, and relationship.

Please post your positive experiences in the
Facilitated Learning Group on LinkedIn.
www.linkedin.com/groups/14108606

If your experience was not all you had hoped,
Contact me, judy@thompsonlanguagecenter.com and/or
share your story on the group link above for support.

ABC Sound Flashcards

38 **illustrated** code words featuring the **sounds** each letter of the alphabet usually makes.
Part One of *ABC Facilitated Reading*
Download printable pdfs of *ABC Facilitated Sound Flashcards,* from
thompsonlanguagecenter.com under the Literacy Tab

ABC Word Flashcards

38 **text only** code **words** introduced in Part One of *ABC Facilitated Reading*. Download printable pdfs of *ABC Facilitated Word Flashcards*, from thompsonlanguagecenter.com under the Literacy Tab

References

[1] www.pbs.org/newshour (*then search*): Why 36 million American adults can't read enough to work — and how to help them;
https://en.wikipedia.org/wiki/Functional_illiteracy

[2] www.readingrockets.org/article/why-some-children-have-difficulties-learning-read

[3] Michael T. Nietzel, "Low Literacy Levels Among U.S. Adults Could Be Costing The Economy $2.2 Trillion A Year," *Forbes*, retrieved 2021-10-16; www.forbes.com (*then search*): Low literacy levels among U.S. adults could be costing the economy $2.2 trillion a year;
https://en.wikipedia.org/wiki/Functional_illiteracy

[4] medium.com/@judysantillipackhem/cant-read-go-directly-to-jail-do-not-pass-go-17f26d286a83

[5] www.mindtools.com/pages/article/forgetting-curve.htm
www.edutopia.org/article/why-students-forget-and-what-you-can-do-about-it

[6] www.smithsonianmag.com (*then search*): Why are Finlands schools successful?;
www.intereconomics.eu (*then search*): The success of the Nordic Countries as a blueprint for small open economies;
Marion Royce, "Study circles in Finland," https://bit.ly/3J9A0fM;
www.weforum.org (*then search*): 10 reasons why Finland's education system is the best in the world

[7] blog.allaboutlearningpress.com/when-two-vowels-go-walking

[8] www.thompsonlanguagecenter.com and Thompson Vowel Chart

[9] https://wind4change.com/4-stages-psychological-safety-timothy-clark-inclusion-learner-contributor-challenger

[10] Kathryn Brillinger. Director, Teaching & Learning at Conestoga College

[11] www.landmarkworldwide.com

[12] www.canr.msu.edu/news/teaching-patterns-to-infants-and-toddlers

[13] ABC Song, https://www.youtube.com/watch?v=75p-N9YKqNo

[14] www.keystoliteracy.com/blog/how-the-brain-learns-to-read

[15] www.goodreads.com/quotes/903747-there-is-no-more-important-homework-than-reading-research-shows

[16] www.logicofenglish.com

[17] www.mybrainware.com

[18] www.dyslexiaida.org

[19] www.livingoutloud.education

[20] www.sciencenews.org/article/balanced-literacy-phonics-teaching-reading-evidence

[21] https://childrenofthecode.org

[22] www.docs.microsoft.com/en-us/typography/develop/word-recognition

[23] www.poetryfoundation.org/poems/44272/the-road-not-taken

www.ingramcontent.com/pod-product-compliance
Lightning Source LLC
Chambersburg PA
CBHW060941170426
43195CB00025B/2991